All About
SPORTS
BETTING

John Gollehon

A PERIGEE BOOK

Perigee Books
are published by
The Berkley Publishing Group
200 Madison Avenue
New York, NY 10016

First Perigee Edition 1989
Copyright © 1986 by Gollehon Publishing Co.

Published simultaneously in Canada

ISBN 0-399-51505-4

Printed in the United States of America
4   5   6   7   8   9   10

CONTENTS

1. **POPULARITY OF
   SPORTS BETTING**   1

2. **THE POINT-SPREAD
   AND MONEY-LINE**   6
   THE POINT-SPREAD   7
   THE MONEY-LINE   8

3. **ODDSMAKERS AND
   BOOKMAKERS**   13
   FOOTBALL "JUICE"   13
   LINE MOVEMENTS   16
   BASEBALL "JUICE"   18
   THE MONEY LINE VS.
      THE POINT-SPREAD   21
   CIRCLED NUMBERS   22
   MAKING THE LINE   23

4. **MAKING YOUR BET**   26
   FOOTBALL   27
   BASKETBALL   29
   BASEBALL   31
   YOUR TICKET   33

5. OTHER BETS   39
   TOTALS   39
   PARLAYS   40
   TEASERS   41
   ROUND ROBIN   42
   HALF-TIME BETS   42
   HOME-RUNS   43
   FUTURE BETS   43
   SPIT BETS   44

6. PICKING WINNERS   45
   MAKE YOUR OWN DECISIONS   45
   THE LINE ON DISCIPLINE   50
   VULNERABILITY   52

7. SECRETS OF A PRO BETTOR   54
   STUDY THE PLAYERS   54
   LINE BIAS   56
   BLOW-OUTS   57
   BET SIZE   58

CHAPTER 1

POPULARITY OF SPORTS BETTING

Sports books in Nevada handle over *one billion dollars* each year in wagers. This is certainly not a "cottage" industry as some players might think. Sports betting is a big business! But if you think $1 billion is big bucks, get ready for this one. The federal government believes that as much as *fifty* billion dollars is wagered each year, *outside* of Nevada! More conservative estimates put the number at thirty billion, but we're still talking numbers that sound more like the budget for NASA. Since sports betting is only legal in Nevada, the 49 *other* billion dollars makes for a lot of unpaid taxes, and a lot of busts.

It should be made clear that the thrust of this book is to the legal side of sports betting in Nevada where the industry has reached unprecedented levels of sophistication, technology, and acceptance. The great majority of sports books today have climbed out of their "chalk on the wall" image and offer the player an attractive, comfortable, and sometimes lavish ambience . . . complete with crystal chandeliers, velvet

1

wallpapering, and cushy carpeting. All a player has to do to get this message is walk through the sports book at Caesars Palace where there are multi-screen projection systems for satellite feeds of three to four games at a time, a 90-foot long computerized display-board for all the betting information, row upon row of plush theater-type seating, adjoining restaurants and bars, and the most sophisticated computer system for recording and monitoring all betting activity. Suffice to say, it's a long way from what it was like twenty years ago.

Of course, not all sports books in Nevada spend $20 million to dress up their walls as Caesars has done. They don't have to. The big lure in Nevada is plainly the fact that sports betting is legal. And that in itself can make it more comfortable. But there are other comparisons to be made with "outstate" operations, and now is as good a time as any.

First and foremost, working with illegal bookmakers can be risky in more ways than one. Indeed, you can't be absolutely sure that you will be paid, especially on sizable amounts. And you certainly can't sue to enforce collection. But when it comes time for *you* to pay, that's a different story. If your losses are big, and you don't fork over, you might feel a little pressure. In fact, many of the major raids are the result of threats from the bookmaker that might scare the player. Instead of paying up, the player simply makes a phone call to the feds telling them where they can find the lost ark of the covenant.

Since most illegal books operate on credit, many players get in over their heads, and have trouble paying off. That's usually when the trouble starts. Even if you are good friends with your "bookie," and trust him to the ends of the earth, sooner or later a dispute always arises. And who do you suppose always wins?

Another disadvantage of illegal bookmakers is, of course, their low visability. They don't advertise in the newspaper. Few players can ever acquire a strong list of sources for shopping and comparing point-spreads, lines, odds, and betting limits. In Las Vegas, the player can choose from over 25 sports books scattered around town; many are on the "strip," and associated with the major hotel/casinos. In Northern Nevada—Reno, Sparks, Carson City, and Lake Tahoe, for example, there are at least half that number ready and willing to take your wager. Although this is not the right time to discuss in detail exactly what you would be shopping for, consider the issue as critical to a winning season. Throughout this book I'll be continually stressing the importance of shopping for the best "deals."

Still another advantage the legal sports book has over the guys out East is that they can be basically fair to everyone by the uniformity of all betting information. Everyone sees the exact same data to decide upon. In contrast, the illegal operation might tailor the lines based on its knowledge of each bettor's traits and tendencies. Perhaps the illegal bookmaker knows that a certain player usually likes home underdogs, or most always bets "totals" over the number.* In these circumstances, don't expect any favors. Over the course of a season, you'll be fighting a losing battle.

Since the figures we cited in our opening paragraph confirm that the great majority of betting activity occurs outside the legal bounds, it poses a problem for so many avid bettors, both large and small. A friend of mine who lives in the Midwest, and an expert foot-

---

*The term "totals" refers to a form of wager whereby the player bets whether or not the total number of points scored in a game by both teams is less than or more than a determined number posted by the sports book. This bet is also referred to as "over and unders."

ball handicapper incidentally, solved his problem by flying to Nevada on Fridays to make his wagers for the weekend. He didn't return until late Monday after the lines went up for the next weekend games. This way, he only had to make his trip every two weeks. Since he was a frequent winner, the trips were like going to work out of town. His large winnings more than paid for his expenses. Of course, only a few players have the luxury (and work schedule) to make such plans. Unless you live in Nevada you really don't have much choice, at least until the time that some other states might legalize sports betting. That's a real possibility, especially in those states where lotteries have been legalized. The extra tax money and stupendous profits for the states are turning a lot of heads. But don't hold your breath.

The idea of betting on sporting events is frowned upon by the team organizations themselves, especially from league headquarters. And it's frowned upon by most churches, except on bingo night. But the encouragement to indeed bet a game or two comes from many unexpected sources. For example, it's virtually impossible to watch a game on television, especially football, where the announcer or pre-game analyst does not mention a betting line. In fact, many so-called experts will brazenly make their selections *against the spread,* just prior to game-time.

During football season, cable TV airs several programs featuring former pro players or sports service personalities rating the weekend games *against the spread,* not unlike critics rating a movie.

Even the newspapers get into the act by publishing the point-spreads for football and basketball and the money-lines for baseball. Many large newspapers include weekly columns featuring their own sportswriters picking the winners *against the spread*. All of this is not because it's so flagrant, but because it's so commonplace.

Before we go on to our next chapter where we'll learn more about Nevada sports books, let's end this chapter by fessing up to why we like to side with the Cowboys, or the Tigers, or the Lakers with a friendly (or not so friendly) wager. I say "we" because I assume you bought this book for reasons other than doing a book report.

For some people, a bet on a game just makes it more "interesting," and that's all. For others, it simply gives them a chance to participate in a contest instead of being a neutral spectator. But some of us like to pick a side, or get down on a nag, or gamble at tennis, golf, or poker because we like to win; we like the challenge of winning. Sure, many people can enjoy the challenge of winning *without* gambling, but for some of us, the "bet" turns a routine event into a serious encounter.

Surprisingly, the amount of the wager is really not the issue. The wager, big or small, has only a secondary meaning. The real issue of gambling is plainly winning or losing. When our team wins, we feel as much a winner as the winning team we bet on.

After a game has been played that you watched, consider your response to someone who asks, "How did your team do?" If you like the winning team, your answer is "They won." If it's your favorite team or alma mater, the answer is "We won." If you had a bet on the team, your answer is "*I* won."

For some people, the betting aspect is the cutting edge between impact and mere fancy.

CHAPTER 2

THE POINT-SPREAD AND MONEY-LINE

For those of you who are not thoroughly familiar with a sports book operation in Nevada, this chapter is for you. You'll learn about the point-spread and money-lines that sports books offer. But not in the greatest detail. We'll save that for later chapters on each of the three most popular games wagered on: football, basketball and baseball. In this way, you won't be overwhelmed by what is a simple, and understandable system that so many new bettors have trouble with at first. Like I said, it's really easy, but it's all in how you present it.

All sports books display their betting information on a large board for everyone to see. As we pointed out in our first chapter, some books are a bit more extravagant than others with computerized displays that flash all the information in lights like a scoreboard. Others "flash" the information with chalk on a plain chalk-board. And still others use a black crayon on a large printed plate of clear plastic. Whether you're in a sports book that uses a chalk-board under hanging fluorescent lights, or one that uses the computerized displays under hanging chandeliers, the numbers themselves should be your only concern. One way or the other, all sports books get their numbers up on the boards. And what you're looking for are the best numbers for *you* based on whether you like the favorite or the underdog.

THE POINT-SPREAD

During football or basketball season, most all sports books offer a "point-spread" to handicap the differences among teams. If, for example, Cleveland is playing Pittsburgh in a football game and you know that Cleveland is a much better team, you can expect to find out that Cleveland is indeed the favorite and will be "giving" a certain number of points to the underdog Steelers. It's no different than when you're playing golf with a friend who is much better than you are. To make the contest a fair opportunity for both, the better player must spot the other a few strokes, depending on exactly how much better your friend really is.

So, getting back to our football game, **if Cleveland is considered to be a touchdown better than Pittsburgh, then Cleveland can be said to be favored by 7 points. The point-spread is 7. And on the board, the number "−7" will be written beside Cleveland's team name,** which is the Browns. Some sports books use only the team names, not the cities, when listing games.

If you bet this game and decide to take Cleveland, you must win by more than 7 points to collect on your bet. If Pittsburgh wins the game outright, or loses by 6 points or less, you've lost your bet. If the game ends up 21-14 Cleveland, there is no decision on the wager and it is returned to you.

It can also be said that Cleveland is "minus 7," or

that Pittsburgh is "plus 7." One or the other, *but not both,* otherwise the point-spread would be 14 points. If the game ends up 14 to 10 with Cleveland winning, you lost your bet if you took Cleveland because with the point-spread taken into account, Pittsburgh "covered the spread." Subtracting 7 points from Cleveland's score gives Pittsburgh the edge 10 to 7. But don't think of the spread in exactly that way. More correctly, think that Cleveland *only won by 4,* and that wasn't enough to cover the spread of 7 points. Don't convert the spread into a different final score than it really was. The score was 14 to 10, and Cleveland didn't cover. That's the way to think it through. If Cleveland had scored *18* points to Pittsburgh's 10, then Cleveland would have indeed covered the spread and you would have won your bet, taking Cleveland −7.

Fortunately, this same rule of the point-spread also applies to basketball games. But unfortunately, it doesn't apply to baseball. Since baseball uses a more complicated way to handicap the teams, we're going to talk baseball a bit more slowly.

THE MONEY-LINE

Baseball betting is based on a "money-line," which is really a means of rating two opposing teams in terms of "odds." Unlike football or basketball where teams are handicapped by a differential in scoring potential as we've just learned, baseball is handicapped on the basis of a team's likelihood of winning, not by how many runs, but just winning.

To make this point absolutely clear, think of football or basketball as being rated in terms of points—how many points is one team better than the other. But in baseball, think of the game as being measured solely by one team's chances of winning, regardless of the final score.

To do this effectively, odds are quoted on the favorite team, such as 7 to 5 odds. And here's just one area where the picture gets a little cloudy. Usually whenever odds are quoted, the first number in the odds expression is the number of times a win will *not* happen. The second number is the number of times it will. The total of both numbers in the odds expression is the total number of theoretical contests it will take to develop a true relationship between winning and losing.

As an example, the odds are 37 to 1 at the roulette table of hitting any one number on the next spin. Since there are 38 compartments on the wheel where the ball might land, you can easily see why the odds are 37 to 1. At the race track, if a horse goes off at 20 to 1, it will be lucky to get out of the starting gate. The bettor has only a one in 21 chance of winning. These examples support the method of quoting odds in virtually all gambling events, the odds *of* winning. But in baseball, sometimes the odds are quoted *against* winning, and the first number in the odds expression may or may not represent the winning events.

So, in the case of our example earlier, where a team is favored by 7 to 5 odds, it means that the favorite should win 7 out of 12 times. The oddsmakers have determined that 12 games are enough to accurately rate the two teams. Seven times the favorite will probably win, and 5 times will probably lose. Of course, we don't know which games will be winners or losers, or for that matter, if the odds will turn out anywhere near what the oddsmakers have predicted, but we can conclude that the favorite has a 58% chance of winning *in each game* of our theoretical set. Yes, some bettors prefer to reduce odds to percentages. In our example, 7/12 is 58% (7 ÷ 12).

Now, let's put names on our two teams and see if we can make any sense out of all this. Let's say the Mets are the favored team, and Boston is the underdog. It's the World Series, and the odds are being quoted on the opening game. The Mets are 7 to 5 favorites over the Sox.

The oddsmakers have also installed the Mets as an 11 to 5 favorite against winning the entire Series. OK, that's easy enough, the Mets have a better than 2 to 1 chance of winning; so they say. If the Series were 16 games instead of the best of 7, the oddsmakers believe the Mets would win 11 times.

But at the beginning of the season, many months prior, these same oddsmakers made the Mets 8 to 1 hopefuls of winning the Series. Does this mean the Mets have an 8 out of 9 chance of winning? Of course not. The oddsmakers were quoting the odds *of* winning, not *against* winning. As a percentage, it's only 11%!

Later in the season, just before the league playoffs, newspapers were correctly quoting the Mets as 5 to 8 favorites of winning the Series. After all, the Mets had the best record in baseball and looked invincible. Although the numbers look "turned around," the expression is correct and follows the same form as the 8 to 1 odds quoted at the beginning of the season. The difference is because the Mets *turned it around* and became the odds-on favorite to win it all.

Seven to 5, 8 to 1, 5 to 8, odds of winning, odds against . . . no wonder the average bettor is confused. If the oddsmakers followed the same odds formula throughout the season, then the Mets would be 5 to 7 favorites over Boston in our opening Series game. But it's quoted as 7 to 5 as if we're asking, "What are the odds that the Mets *won't* win it?" Are you still with me?

From Odds to Dollars

Converting the odds to a money-line is no cinch either. Here's the way most beginners do it. Let's consider our 7 to 5 odds as being $70 to $50. Now, let's double the numbers to $140 to $100, same relationship, same odds. Sports books put up the betting numbers on a basis of $100, or just "100." If the Mets are indeed a 7 to 5 favorite, up goes the number "140" beside their name on the board. A minus sign is in front of the number to indicate that they are the favorite.

Now, if we're going to bet the Mets, assuming you still want to, we must give the sports book $140 to win $100, or any other amount to be paid in that same ratio. We can wager $70 to win $50, or even $7 to win $5, although that paltry amount might be under the minimum they accept. Seven dollars just doesn't turn anyone on anymore, especially in Las Vegas.

The best way to convert the "– 140" on the board is the same way the sports books themselves do it. Think of it as – $1.40 and figure that you can win $1 on every $1.40 you risk. Give the sports book $14; if the Mets win, you win $10 (plus your original $14 is given back of course).

If you like the underdog Sox, you would ideally like to bet $1 to win $1.40 and that would make it a fair proposition. Of course, the sports book wouldn't earn any profit over the long term doing it that way, so he adjusts the actual numbers so that he can make an "honest" living. He'll ask you to risk a little more on the favorite, and take a little less on the underdog. This way the poor guy can feed his kids.

Incidentally, if you get your preliminary numbers out of the newspapers, chances are they'll be listed in a very strange way such as 6½-7. To make any sense out of *these* numbers simply insert a "5" between them and read it as 7 to 5 for the favorite and 6½ to 5 for the underdog. The second number, not the first, represents the favorite . . . apparently another scheme to confuse the bettor. In our example, the difference between 7 and 6½ is the bookie's "adjustment" as we called it, or "juice" as it's commonly called, and represents his profit. But don't worry about juice now. We'll cover that in the next chapter. Always save some of your worries for later.

If you're reading this book in early summer, during baseball season, you're probably saying to yourself, "Gosh, I wish this was the football season!" And you're right. Baseball is indeed more confusing, and might help to explain why the action is not nearly as great as football or basketball.

To recap, when you get the betting line on baseball, you might get it: 8 to 5, −160, minus a buck-sixty, or 7½-8. But they all mean the same thing. You must bet $8 to win $5 if you like the favored team. Unlike football or basketball, you must bet more to win less if you like the favorite, and bet less to win more if you like the underdog.

CHAPTER 3

ODDSMAKERS AND BOOKMAKERS

"Oddsmaker" and "bookmaker" are terms that the betting public sometimes confuse. An oddsmaker only makes a betting line; the bookmaker "books" the bets. Sometimes an oddsmaker is also a bookmaker; but not all bookmakers are oddsmakers. They have nothing to do with butchers, bakers, and candlestick-makers.

Wait a minute!

A bookmaker is often referred to as a "BM" although if I were a bookmaker, I certainly wouldn't want to be called that. In Nevada, a bookmaker is most often referred to as a sports book or race book, depending on whether it takes action on sporting events, horse-racing, or both. Throughout this text, I'm going to refer to the bookmaker as a sports book since we're only interested in sports betting activity in Nevada, where it's legal.

FOOTBALL "JUICE"

Like a casino operation, the sports book itself does not actually gamble, or at least would prefer not to. A casino offers gambling, but the gambling is done on the part of the players, not by the casino. Since all games have a particular house advantage, the more players play, the more the casino wins. Over a long term, the casino never loses.

The sports book operation is set up along these same lines, and with rare exception, never loses over the long term either. It's a function of the quantity of bettors, the accuracy of the lines, and of course, good management.

In order to establish a "house edge," the sports book requires that all wagers on football and basketball (all games based on a point-spread) are made at 11 to 10 odds. This means that all bets, whether for the favorite or the underdog, must be made "against the odds," in addition to against the point-spread. For example, if you want to bet $100, a winning selection will earn you $90.90 based on 11 to 10 odds. If you want to *win* $100, you must risk $110. To avoid the confusing payoffs, always make your bets in consideration of the 11 to 10 odds, such as $55 to win $50, $11 to win $10, or $220 to win $200. Regardless of the size of your bet, always remember that you're betting against the odds, and against the point-spread.

Here's how the 11 to 10 odds looks on paper. Reducing the sports book's action to two players, one taking each side laying $110, you can see that the sports book is holding $220 (called the "handle"). Assuming the final score is not the exact point-spread, and that the betting line did not move, the sports book will pay one winner $100 and return the $110 wager. What the sports book has left is its profit of $10. **As a percentage, its profit is 4½% (10 ÷ 220).**

BETTOR A	BETTOR B	SPORTS BOOK
BETS $110 ON TEAM 1	**BETS** $110 ON TEAM 2	**HOLDS** $220
WINS $100	**LOSES BET**	**NETS** $10
+110*		
$210		

*Bet returned

It's obvious that if the opening line correctly split the bettor's opinion, and the sports book indeed received equal 2-way action, it earns the juice *no matter which team wins.*

Many new bettors, aware that they have to bet 10% more than they can win, incorrectly assume that the percentage against them is 10%. As you can see, the actual percentage must be based over the course of both probabilities: win or lose. Experienced players who know this still believe that the true percentage is 5%, but of course that number is wrong also, as we've just proven. We can assume their error is using $200 as the handle instead of the actual $220.

Since many new bettors are surprised that the juice is "only" 4½%, let's prove it again a different way, the same way that most casino-game percentages are determined. At the roulette table for example, if the correct odds are 37 to 1 for hitting any one number, yet the casino will only pay 35 to 1, we simply divide the number of units the casino has "shorted" us (2) by the total of both numbers in the correct odds expression (38). Two divided by 38 is 5.26%, which is the percentage against the player at roulette. Similarly, when betting football, we are "shorted" 1/11 of a unit. Divided by the total of both numbers in the correct odds expres-

sion (the correct odds are obviously 1 to 1) we yield the
same 4½%.

$$\frac{\frac{1}{11}}{2} = \frac{1}{11} \cdot \frac{1}{2} = \frac{1}{22} = .045$$

LINE MOVEMENTS

Earlier, we mentioned that the sports book will earn
its 4½% juice only if the betting line has not moved,
and if an equal number of dollars are bet on both sides.
If either criterion is not met (it rarely is), the sports book
might win more, win less, or actually lose. In other
words, the sports book is gambling. Of course, we
would also have to assume that the final score did not
rest exactly on the point-spread. Now, let's analyze each
aspect of all this to see how any variations can affect
the sports book's profits, and perhaps the bettor's profits too.

If the opening line is not on target, the sports book
will not get equal 2-way betting action, which of course
is what it wants. If indeed the opening line was not
perfectly suited for 2-way equal action, the sports book's
option is to adjust the line. If too much money is coming in on the favorite, it might make the spread a half-
point or even one full point higher to discourage more
betting on the favorite and increase the action on the
underdog. Once the betting action begins to right itself,
the sports book might again adjust the line by moving
it back down, but only if the action warrants. Since
some sports books accept wagers of $10,000 (or more)
on regular season football games, you can see that only

a few bets, if all one-sided, can quickly make the line move. It's not unusual for a football line to move two points when the action gets heavy. In that case, a large line movement is not necessarily because the line was wrong at the outset, but could be caused by unusually heavy one-sided betting by only two or three players.

Accordingly, the player might find different lines by shopping the many sports books available. Indeed, shopping for the best line is critical to a successful bettor. As we mentioned, differences of 2 points or more are not that unusual. The line movement might help the sports book by balancing the money on both sides, but it also might help certain bettors by giving them less points to lay on a favorite, or more points to take on the underdog, depending on which direction the line actually moves.

Middled or Sided

Although the sports book moves a betting line in its own best interests, sometimes it backfires, and ends up costing the sports book huge sums of cash. Here's how it can happen. Let's say Dallas opens at -6 against Detroit. Early betting is brisk and most of it is on Dallas. To counter this one-sided action, the sports book decides to move the line all the way to -8. If a bettor took Dallas at -6 before the line moved, and then took the underdog Lions at $+8$, what do you suppose would happen if the game ended up 28-21 Dallas? What happens is the bettor wins both bets! The bookie got "middled," as the term is called, but a more appropriate term for it is "killed!" That's the risk the sports book takes when line movements are significant.

Incidentally, the sports book is also vulnerable to losing one side and "pushing" on the other (pushing means a tie). That would be the case in our example if the final score was either a 6-point or 8-point win for Dallas. In this instance, the sports book is said to have been "sided."

If the betting line did not move, and the point-spread did not include a half-point, it's possible that the entire contest is a push. If the point-spread is 10, and the final score has the favorite winning by 10, the sports book has to return *all* the bets. No action, no profit.

BASEBALL "JUICE"

In baseball, where a money-line is used instead of a point-spread, the sports book has tailored the structure of the odds payouts so that it earns a profit over long-term action. If the betting line is −140 for the favorite, the underdog will go off at +130, not +140. In theory, the sports book breaks even when the favorite wins, and wins when the underdog wins. If only two players take action on a game, each player taking a different side but at the same betting level, you can see by our chart that follows how the sports book will fare.

BETTOR A	BETTOR B	SPORTS BOOK
BETS $140 ON FAVORITE	BETS $100 ON UNDERDOG	HOLDS $240
	FAVORITE WINS AT −140	

WINS $100
  + 140*
  $240
	LOSES BET	BREAKS EVEN

	UNDERDOG WINS AT +130	

LOSES BET	WINS $130
	  + 100*
	  $230
		NETS $10

*Bet returned

In theory, the dogs pay the juice, but sometimes it doesn't all work out as it should on paper. Yes, a sports book from time to time does indeed take a financial risk. Live by the sword . . . .

Before we go on to the next chapter, we should find out exactly how much juice the sports book makes during the baseball season, and compare this to basketball and football. This discussion is easily the most boring part of the book, but it will help you identify the lines in terms of the edge against you.

All baseball lines are not all the same. I'm not talking about the actual numbers, but the juice that's in the numbers. Sure, the numbers do vary and that's important in terms of shopping for the best numbers. But the differences in the numbers also vary, specifically the difference between a favorite and underdog team. That difference, if you recall, is the sports book's profit. And it's worth shopping for also.

Let's say our line on the Mets/Red Sox game is −140 Mets, +130 Sox. This line is called a "dime-line" in sports book parlance, meaning that the difference between what the favorite *takes* from the bettor and what the underdog *gives* to the bettor is 10 cents. Remember to assess the line as −$1.40 and +$1.30 for simplicity sake and the 10 cents will become more evident.

Some sports books might offer a 15-cent line or 20-cent line instead, and you can be assured it means more profit for the sports book and less for the players. In our example, to make the line 15 cents the favorite Mets might be listed at −145 and the Sox at +130, or perhaps the extra juice will come from the underdog as −140 Mets and +125 Sox.

In order for the sports book to hold its percentages constant, more or less, the 10-cent betting line will become 20 cents when the favorite goes over −200 (becomes greater than a 2 to 1 favorite). In fact, the 10-cent line becomes a 15-cent line at −200 in order to prevent the sports book's profit from falling below 1%. The reason for this variation is not to deceive the bettor, nor to confuse him, but simply to maintain a reasonable profit level for the sports book.

As you can appreciate, if the difference between the numbers remained the same, while the numbers themselves became larger, then the percentage of difference would become *smaller*. The adjustment in the line is merely to prevent this from happening.

But don't be so naive as to think that all sports books follow this same schedule. It always pays to shop for the best numbers, *and* the best percentages.

Proving the Juice

LINE	ACTION
METS −140	BETTOR A LAYS THE ODDS AT $140
SOX +130	BETTOR B TAKES THE ODDS AT $100

SPORTS BOOK IS HOLDING $240,
IF UNDERDOG WINS, SPORTS BOOK NETS $10.
IF FAVORITE WINS, SPORTS BOOK BREAKS EVEN.

$$\frac{10}{240} = .04 \qquad \frac{.04}{2} = .02 = 2\% \text{ JUICE}$$

In determining the sports book's actual juice in baseball, we follow the same procedure as in football, except we must divide our number in half since the juice is only earned when the underdog wins. Over the long-term, the underdog wins about half the time. In football, the juice is applied to *both* sides of a game, and earned regardless which side wins.

Baseball's juice computation reminds me of baccarat, where the "juice" is only applied to the banker-hand, *and only when it wins*. The hand is one of two nearly equal possibilities. Assuming the hand is bet about half the time, and indeed wins about half the time, we divide the juice of 5% by 4 (½ of ½), not 2, in order to approximate its actual cost to the player.

Baccarat belongs in the same breath with 10-cent baseball because it's the player's best game overall in the casino percentage-wise. Similarly, a 10-cent baseball line is the bettor's best game in the sports book, percentage-wise.

THE MONEY-LINE VS. THE POINT-SPREAD

Now we know that the sports book makes about 2½% or less (2% average) on a 10-cent baseball line. If the line is 20 cents, the sports book will make about 4½%, or approximately the same as football and basketball. Yes, in terms of percentages, baseball's 10-cent line is more attractive than football or basketball, but doesn't get anywhere near the overall action, in spite of the percentages, and the length of the season, and the number of games.

Why not give baseball a point-spread you ask, as if to suggest that the sports books must all be run by a bunch of morons. Well, it's been tried, but not successfully. And here's why.

First, baseball is a relatively low-scoring affair. It's difficult to pick a number that would equally divide the betting public. Secondly, there is more parity in baseball that would make point-spreads unattractive. Thirdly, baseball has been based on odds, not points, since the days of Abner Doubleday. Sports books that have tried a baseball point-spread are plainly going against the grain.

And it works the other way too. Football and basketball would not be successfully wagered with a money-line. Unlike baseball where most all teams have a reasonable chance of winning a particular contest, basketball and football games are full of blow-outs— teams with virtually no chance of winning. Such mismatches are most evident in college football where scores of 56-0 are not uncommon. With a money-line, who would want to take the underdog regardless of the odds payout. Even at +1000, or some such unheard of number, a team that could easily lose by 50+ points is not going to get my attention, or interest, or money! Even if the skies parted above South Bend, and Slippery Rock's players rode in on golden chariots . . . I'll still take Notre Dame!

But what if Slippery Rock got some points. Lots of points. Not odds. Points! Indeed, the point-spread can "even-up" virtually any two teams on the betting board. But sometimes the mismatches are so severe that the sports book doesn't want to offer it at *any* number. In such cases, the game goes off the board and only the teams slug it out. Today, it would be unusual to find a football or basketball point-spread on the board at 40 points or more, unless it's "circled."

CIRCLED NUMBERS

A circled point-spread number means the sports book

will take only limited action on that particular game. If there's any doubt about critical factors, such as a quarterback injury or bad weather, the betting limit might be greatly reduced. Similarly, if the game is a meaningless contest or if the teams are greatly mismatched, up goes the circle and down goes the bets. The sports book is simply protecting itself.

In some severe cases, the game might go off the board as indicated by an "X" in place of the point-spread, meaning that the game cannot be bet, at any amount. And here's another good reason for shopping. An "X" on the board in one sports book doesn't necessarily mean the game's off all over town, but that's probably what you'll find.

MAKING THE LINE

There's a lot of intrigue involved in the actual making of a line for football, basketball, or baseball. Who does it? How is it tested? How accurate is it?

Prior to 1950 when sports betting was not against state or federal law in much of the country, two or three well-known oddsmakers of the era made the lines that were distributed all over the land for bookies in every hamlet to use. Rarely would a local bookmaker put up his own numbers for fear of a costly mistake. His profit picture had a direct bearing on the accuracy of the lines.

After federal law put the whammy on the oddsmaker's grapevine, most of the larger operations were moved to Canada or to Las Vegas where the flow of betting information continued, law or no law. Local bookmakers needed the oddsmaker's expertise, no matter where they were. Without the oddsmakers, local bookies were at the mercy of their own bettors.

By the early 1960s, betting lines were issued almost exclusively from Las Vegas. By 1963, sports books in Nevada were taking notice of a knowledgeable man who had just moved to Las Vegas from the East Coast. His name was Bob Martin, and by 1967 he had settled in at Churchill Downs, a sports book operation on the famed Las Vegas Strip. Martin's line had fast become the accepted standard, posted on the boards by virtually all other sports books in town.

In 1972, Martin moved to the Union Plaza, and the source of the betting lines moved with him. He continued working his magic until 1982 when he retired from the hectic pace and constant scrutiny. Today, no one argues the fact that Bob Martin was the best oddsmaker of them all.

After his retirement, betting lines were posted by individual sports books when it became apparent that no single oddsmaker could step in. Without a "General," the army of sports books were marching in different directions.

Even today, the betting lines are a result of a consortium of oddsmakers in Nevada who no longer try to beat the other sports books to the punch, but would rather see a unified, tested, and accepted line from which all can serve their customers.

In the past, the oddsmakers tested their lines by allowing an elite group of shrewd bettors to "play" their lines, and report back on their opinions. During the 50s and 60s, it was an accepted notion that this elite group of bettors were in Miami, but in fact, many were from Chicago and Minneapolis. If these smart bettors found an error in the lines, they would tell the oddsmakers. In exchange for their "services," they were allowed to play the original line with the uncorrected errors. Today however, the "smart" bettors are in Nevada and do indeed report to the oddsmakers as part of the consensus opinion, but they rarely get first shot during a line's formative stages.

It should be pointed out that betting lines are not as stable as they were in the past, especially when Bob Martin was at the helm. Line movements can be quite severe on Mondays when the lines are first posted during football season, and the avid bettor must be quick to find any mistake. Within hours, the sports book will know exactly how successful his line is, and *within minutes* will make any needed changes. Most often, the line will become rock-solid by midday, and continue through the week—numbers that remarkably, week after week, split the betting public right down the middle.

CHAPTER 4

MAKING YOUR BET

Up to this point, I've tried to prepare you for actually walking into a sports book, reading the board, and making your wager like you've been doing it for years. You already know about the baseball money-line, and the point-spread for football and basketball. You now know how the sports book operates, its profit objective, and the player's options.

If you're not in full understanding of the previous chapters, go back and read them again. I've carefully structured the information in this book so that you won't be blasted with data all at one time. Sports betting is both simple and complicated. There's nothing worse than getting into it with a "little" bit of knowledge. In fact that's true of just about anything. Promise me that you won't bet a single dollar until you fully understand what you're doing, have shopped for the best lines and percentages, and will only bet those games that you have a very strong feeling about, with money that you can comfortably afford to lose. There are no guarantees, my friend, no matter how well you have prepared. Be careful. With that understanding, let's do it.

FOOTBALL

The season begins in August for the professionals with "exhibition" games, that only a fool would bet. College games begin in September and continue until the bowl games on New Year's. The pro season ends with the Super Bowl usually set for mid-January.

Here's a typical board-listing for a professional game:

21 Detroit Lions

10:00   44

22 Chicago Bears – 10

The time of kick-off is listed to the left and is generally in the order of the games to be played that day. In other words, the late games will be listed last. Incidentally, most sports books will accept wagers right up until kick-off, especially if the game is shown on its closed-circuit TV screen.

The numbers shown to the left of the team names are the sports book's numerical listings that help to keep the games in order and assist the ticket writer in locating the team (and the point-spread) of the game you wish to bet.

Team listings will always have the home team on the bottom. In our example, we can see that the game is being played at Soldier Field in Chicago. The " – 10" to the right of the Bears tells us that the Bears are in fact favored to win by 10 points. You can either "lay" the 10 points and take the Bears, or "take" the 10 points with the Lions. Although it's not shown on the listing, you can assume the Lions are " + 10" as the underdog in this contest. If you bet the Bears, they must win the game by *more than* 10 points. If you like the Lions, you will win the bet if either the Lions win, or if the Bears win by *less than* 10 points. If the game ends up a 10-point difference in favor of the Bears, your wager will be returned to you as a "push," meaning a tie. You neither win nor lose.

Pick 'Em

Sometimes two teams will be evenly matched. When this happens, the term "Pick," "Pick 'Em," or simply "PK" will be shown on the board in place of a point-spread number.

In the case of a pick 'em game, you will lay 11 to 10, as usual, on either team to win outright . . . no points either way. A tie game in this case is a push; your bet will be refunded.

But remember, the oddsmaker doesn't necessarily believe the teams are evenly matched in a pick 'em game, but that *the betting public believes* the teams are evenly matched. That's a big difference sometimes. What's really important in pick 'em contests, or any games with a point-spread for that matter, is whether or not you believe the line truly reflects the scoring potential of two opposing teams. If it doesn't, in your humble opinion, then you've found a game worth considering.

The "Totals"

The number "44" to the right of our listing is the "totals" number for betting over or under on the combined final score for *both* teams. If you believe the game will be a low scoring contest, you would bet "under" 44. If you think the offenses will generate a lot of points, you would logically bet "over" 44. If you don't have the slightest idea how many points might be scored, then don't bet it! If the total score lands exactly on 44, all bets, either over or under, are returned to the player.

Betting on either the favorite or underdog, or betting the totals, the player must wager at 11 to 10 odds, meaning that you must always give the sports book more than you would expect to win. If you would like to win $100, you must risk $110. To make the payouts easy, always be in multiples of 11, such as $11 to win $10, $22 to win $20, $55 to win $50, and so on.

BASKETBALL

Professional basketball teams begin their exhibition season in October, while college teams begin action in November. The pros play until the NBA tournament (a season all by itself), and the college season ends in March when the NCAA tournament is held. Incidentally, many of the early season college games are gross mismatches with strong national powers taking on struggling small-college teams. It's the time when either the games are taken off the betting boards or smart bettors beat up on their bookie. In sports book parlance, these "smart" bettors are called "wise guys," and their betting action can greatly affect betting lines, regardless of the size of their wagers. As a general rule, pro action receives little attention from the wise guys until later in the season when the teams have shown their true colors. Similarly, when the college season approaches the new year (a time of holiday tournaments), conference play begins and the selections become less predictable. Generally, teams within a conference are more evenly matched.

Here's a typical board-listing for a professional game:

63 Boston Celtics – 6½

12:00   220

64 Atlanta Hawks

As you no doubt recall, betting basketball is exactly like football. It's against the point-spread and you must lay 11 to 10 odds to win.

Just like our football listing, the tip-off time is listed to the left, and the "totals" number is shown on the far right. The Celtics are favored to win by 6½ points, and the game is being played at Atlanta.

Half-Points

The ½-point in the betting line insures that the game will not fall exactly on the spread. At this number, all bets will be either won or lost . . . no ties. If Boston wins the game by 6 points, and you bet Atlanta, you'll win the bet by only a half-point! But by the same token, all the bettors who took Boston will *lose* by a half-point.

If indeed you lost the game by a half-point, you might as well have lost it by 20! A loss is a loss. And don't make excuses for your lousy luck by blaming it on some poor player who threw up an air-ball in the closing seconds, or who couldn't make just one of two free-throws to save it for you. *You'll win some games that you should have lost, and you'll lose some games that you should have won.* Sports betting is a microcosm of life's ups and downs, good luck and bad luck, successes and failures. Accept your losses as easily as you accept your wins and you'll be a better player for it, in all of life's little games.

BASEBALL

The national pastime is a 7-month affair, stretching from early April to the World Series in October. There are games played nearly every day, and the betting action can turn into a regular "grind," especially for "locals" who live in Nevada. In fact, most pro-bettors believe the season is *too* long, from a betting standpoint, where inexperienced bettors soon become overwhelmed by the multitude of games. Baseball can take a bettor's money faster than any other game. Go easy during the baseball season, making sure your stake will "stretch" throughout the season.

Here's a typical board-listing for a professional game:

	11 Boston Red Sox	Hurst	−130	
4:30				8
	12 Detroit Tigers	Morris	+120	

This game gets underway at 4:30 in Las Vegas (7:30 p.m. in Detroit), and will be played at Tiger Stadium as evidenced by the Tigers being listed second. Unlike football or basketball, the betting line lists team personnel, namely the pitchers expected to start the game. In addition, a money-line is posted instead of a point-spread, making the Red Sox favored in this contest and the Tigers are the underdog. The number at the far right represents the total number of runs for betting the totals "over and under."

The Pitchers

The reason that the pitchers are listed on the board

should be obvious once you realize how important the pitchers are to the outcome of a baseball game. In no other game is one player so important; in fact, no other player on the team is as important as the pitcher. In setting the lines, the oddsmaker must carefully weigh each pitcher's record and recent performance. So must the bettor. For example, if a rookie just called up from Crockett's Bluff got the starting nod instead of Hurst—one of their best pitchers—we can safely assume that the betting odds for the Sox would not only go down, but possibly shift the Sox to the underdog side of the ledger. That's how important the starting pitchers are. A baseball bettor must have more than just a good understanding of the teams; he must have solid information about the pitchers themselves. The pitchers carry the teams. Make no mistake.

If we are going to bet baseball like the pros do, we must always ask for "listed pitchers," when making our wager. This term means that our bet is on *only* if the two starting pitchers listed actually start the contest. If not, then we don't want the bet! Inexperienced bettors who show no concern about the pitchers (and obviously no concern about their money) make their bets in "action," meaning that the bet goes regardless of who's pitching. Not smart.

The Payoff

In reviewing the money-line once again, we must bet $130 to win $100 if we like the Red Sox. If we like the Tigers, we stand to win $120 on a wager of $100 if the Tigers win. Remember that the minus-sign indicates the favorite, and the plus-sign identifies the underdog.

Of course, we can make the wagers in any amount

above the sports book's minimum which is usually $5 or $10. But the payoffs will be in the same ratio as the odds.

An easy way to compute your own payoffs on the favorite team is to simply divide your bet by the number on the board reduced to a dollar and change. Using our −130 number as an example, and a bet of $20, our payoff will be $15.38.

$$\frac{\$20}{\$1.30} = \$15.38$$

If we're betting the underdog Tigers at +120 with a wager of $20, we change the +120 to $1.20 and multiply times your wager to get our payoff.

$$\$20 \times \$1.20 = \$24$$

As you can see, betting the favorite you'll win a dollar on every $1.30 you wager. And betting the underdog you'll win $1.20 on every dollar you bet.

YOUR TICKET

Unlike an illegal bookmaker who usually takes a bettor's credit, Nevada sports books require *cash* at the window. In some cases, credit can indeed be established at Nevada sports books, but the stiff requirements, including minimum deposits and residency, usually preclude the small or out-of-town bettor from participating. In addition, there is some concern presently as to the merits and safeguards of the phone-account credit system.

In any event, assuming the bettor is playing with cash, a receipt for his wager is a "ticket" that might be hand-written or computer-printed. The ticket is more than a receipt however. If the ticket wins, or part of the ticket wins, it's almost as good as cash. Give your tickets the same respect.

First and foremost, be sure that your ticket is marked exactly as you intended it to be. Check it carefully *before* you leave the betting window. If there is a mistake on the ticket, it will be difficult to make any corrections at a later date. At the very least, it will be a time-consuming mess.

Check the ticket to be sure the correct team(s) is listed as your pick (remember that most all sports books use the team name, not the city, such as Lakers instead of Los Angeles); that your wager is correct (some sports books list either the wager, the winning amount, or both); and that the odds, point-spread, or money-line is exactly as the board shows.

Once your ticket is printed, you'll have locked in the odds or point-spread, even if the numbers change after you leave the window. The exception is in baseball when an "action" ticket is played and the listed pitchers do not start.

With so many games on the board, the ticket writer will ask that you identify your selections by number. All teams have a corresponding number assigned, and this makes it easier for the writer to find the game and confirm the odds or point-spread. In the case of computers keeping track of all betting action, the numbering system is an absolute must. Today, everything is a number.

Another matter to consider when making your wager is timing. During the football season, if you make your plays on Sunday morning you can expect to stand in line. The same is true for Saturday football contests in the college ranks. Use common sense. Avoid the hectic pace of the sports book during these busy times if you can . . . unless you're waiting and hoping for the lines to change at the last minute.

Cashing Your Winning Ticket

It would be pointless to tell you when the sports books' betting windows are open since the times vary among the shops. Generally, those associated with casino-hotels are open longer. The same is true of the cashier's window where winning tickets are paid. In the case of a late game, you might have to wait until the next morning to be paid.

It is also impossible to define the time-limits on cashing a ticket, because this rule varies among sports books also. In most cases, there is a 30 day period in which you can cash the ticket. Some shops will go 90 days; others might give you a year. Always be sure you know all the rules before you wager.

Another interesting rule that hopefully you'll never have to worry about concerns lost tickets. In most cases, if you report the lost ticket giving the sports book all the information about it, you'll be protected. At least to the extent that the sports book will be very careful if the ticket is presented for payment. They will want to be sure of the rightful owner.

If the ticket is not presented, chances are good that you'll be paid. But why take the chance. Like I said, treat the ticket as cash, and be sure you have a full understanding of the terms that go with it. To a degree, the sports book has the upper hand because they're holding your cash. Nonetheless, most all sports books will do whatever possible to make you happy. They're not out to lose customers.

If you're an out-of town player, most all sports books will accept mail delivery of your ticket and will remit the winnings by return mail. But check it out first. For example, Harrah's in Reno clearly states on their tickets: "WAGERS HONORED FOR ONE YEAR. WAGERS WILL NOT BE PAID BY MAIL." Of course, not only are the rules different among casinos, they also change. The smart bettor must learn how to read "the fine print," and ask questions when in doubt.

Assuming the sports book will indeed accept a winning ticket by mail, it's a good idea to include a stamped, self-addressed envelope along with the ticket. This practice might speed your money along to you. Most sports books recommend that you mail the ticket by registered mail and insure it for its value. You should also write your name on the ticket before you mail it, but you should do this anyhow, immediately upon receipt, even if you plan to present the ticket in person. In this way, a lost ticket will be tougher to cash by a dishonest person. Unfortunately, many bettors elect not to write their name on the ticket because they don't want the sports book personnel to know who they are, for a host of reasons. Still, it's good advice.

Pro-bettors will also write down the serial number of the ticket, and all the relevant information, and keep that slip of paper in a different location from where the ticket is kept. More good advice.

Giving Your Name

Don't be surprised or upset if the ticket writer asks

for your name and address when you submit a large amount of cash. The new Nevada regulation, 6A, requires that sports books report large cash transactions to the Treasury Department. Most often, the sports book will try to keep track of large bets, even those under the $10,000 minimum amount for reporting, in case the bettor has more than one ticket played within 24 hours. If you refuse to give your name and address on amounts under $10,000, at the very least the ticket writer will jot down your description: height, weight, color of eyes and hair, etc. On amounts over $10,000, if you refuse to give your vitals they won't accept your wager. That simple.

The idea behind regulation 6A is to discourage the "laundering" of illegal money in Nevada; changing little bills into big bills and so on. Everyone has to play by this rule, although no one likes it, especially the sports books themselves because of all the extra paperwork involved.

No Action

There are times when your ticket might be declared "no action" and the wager refunded. In both basketball and football, if for some reason the game is not completed, your ticket might be refunded. Check with the sports book to determine its rules on this matter. Ask how long the game must go on, or at what point in the contest is the game considered "official" by the sports book's standard.

If a significant change in the game's conditions occurs, your ticket might again be voided. A change in the date, or location, is usually reason enough to refund on all wagers.

Baseball is a bit different because there are a host of reasons for refunding on a ticket. As you recall from our previous discussion on baseball, if the bettor wants "listed" pitchers as he should, and the starting pitcher (one or the other) is different than listed, the bet is off.

Virtually all sports books require that baseball games last at least 4½ innings to be considered official, except in the case of totals where the game must go the full distance. If a game is suspended in extra innings with the score tied at the end of the last completed inning, your bet is refunded even if the game is rescheduled for a later date. If a dispute arises, such as a team's protest of the outcome, the decision that day usually is official for betting purposes, even if a later ruling reverses the outcome. On this and all other rules, you must verify with the ticket writer. Don't take any other advice. Get it from the source!

CHAPTER 5

OTHER BETS

All three sports that we are concerned with: football, baseball, and basketball, offer the bettor a host of betting propositions other than simply picking against the money-line in baseball, or against the point-spread in football and basketball. Virtually all pro-bettors concentrate exclusively on simply picking the winning teams. For the most part, they leave the other bets to the suckers. We're not going to dwell on these other bets because they really should not be recommended. But since they are a part of sports betting, this book would be incomplete without at least a cursory discussion.

TOTALS

Since we've already explained the concept of betting on the final score, as being "over" or "under" a particular number, there's no need to give you more examples. However, you should be made aware that the conditions on which a final score rests are very difficult to measure. Accordingly, most experienced bettors consider the totals as a frivolous wager and ignore that part of the betting line. The only possible exception is in professional basketball where the scoring potential of such few key players is more easily judged. Incidentally, most sports books do not set totals on most college games, for obvious reasons. If the oddsmakers would have difficulty coming up with the numbers, what chance would the bettor have?

PARLAYS

If you want to show everyone in the sports book parlor that you're a rank amateur, walk up to the betting window and ask about making a parlay bet. But be careful. The guy might try to sell you a bridge, or a deed to a lost gold mine. Actually, the "gold mine" deal might be better for you.

A parlay is nothing more than combining two or more games (usually up to 10) on one bet, in the hopes you'll win them all and . . . well, own your own gold mine. The payoff for picking 10 out of 10 winners is enticing. But like the million dollar slot jackpots and the $50,000 prize in keno, you're bucking big odds against you. A "realistic" parlay bet of two games should pay at 3 to 1 odds. Picking two winners out of two is indeed 3 to 1 odds.

$$(2 \times 2) - 1 \text{ to } 1$$

Your payoff on a two-game parlay however is 13 to 5, not the true 15 to 5 odds that you should be paid. The difference is juice, and plenty of it. How much? If the correct odds are 15 to 5 (3 to 1), yet we are only paid *13* to 5, we are shorted 2 units out of 20 (15 + 5).

$$\frac{2}{20} = .10 = 10\% \text{ juice!}$$

The odds against you climb even higher when you pick more games. Forget it!

Many sports books associated with casino-hotels distribute "parlay cards" throughout the casino, much like keno tickets. The cards list a selection of upcoming games (usually football), and all the player must do is mark his picks—against the spread of course—then sit back and watch his money disappear through the casino's "black hole." In most cases, ties lose. And if one game loses, the whole card is a loser. Such a deal!

The parlay card gimmick has been tried, or is being considered, by several states outside of Nevada as part of a legalized sports betting program, similar to state lotteries. Delaware gave it a shot in 1976, but it lasted only a few weeks because of a lot of snags, not the least of which was an NFL lawsuit against Delaware for "contaminating the game of football." But that's another story. I'm biting my tongue to spare you my own personal convictions about such narrow-minded thinking on the part of team owners and league executives. I won't preach "morality" to you, and I don't want anyone preaching it to me!

To sum up, avoid parlays not because you're "contaminating" a sport, but because you're contaminating your wallet!

TEASERS

Here's another bet that's similar to a parlay, but the sports book will let you add points to the point-spread (or subtract points) to make your picks stronger. What you are allowed to do is called "moving the line." The number of points you can move is usually 6 points in football and 4 points in basketball. If Dallas is favored over St. Louis by 10 points, you can take Dallas at −4 instead, or take St. Louis at +16! Sounds good, right?

Wrong! As you might expect by now, the payoffs are worse than the parlays. Instead of the true odds of 15 to 5, you might get 9 to 5. Juice? I'm not even going to figure it out. Yes, ties lose . . . and you'll lose your shirt, pants, socks and anything else of value if you're "teased" by these stupid bets.

ROUND ROBIN

Are you ready for this one? You can select up to four games, and parlay any two or any three, or go for all four winners. This reminds me of marking a "combination way ticket" in the keno parlor. And that's where it belongs. If you win two out of three, you might get a 3 to 5 payoff. On $5 you get $3! Is this legal?

HALF-TIME BETS

You guessed it. At half-time, the sports book will put up some new numbers for the second half, as if the second half was an entirely new game. It's a great way for the bettor to get his money back if the game isn't going exactly as he had planned. And it's a great way to lose twice the money you originally risked. The sports books are playing on the gambler's greed, a way to get back earlier losses. These guys are always looking for ways to take your money.

The danger of half-time betting should be obvious to anyone who's watched at least one football game in his entire lifetime. Have you ever watched a team get blown out in the first half, then come back and win it in the stretch? It's all a function of the coaches' famous half-time speeches. With half-time bets, we are not only concerned with rating the teams and the players, but now we have to rate the coaches. Incidentally, never make half-time bets against Notre Dame. The coach has his own speech-writer.

HOME-RUNS

To make this bet work for you, consult an astrological chart or get out your old ouija-board. It's really that silly. Surprisingly, a few sports books in Northern Nevada, and very few in Las Vegas are offering the home-run bet, based on a money-line such as − 190 Kansas City and + 170 Baltimore. Yes, it's a 20-cent line and "KC" is expected to hit more out of the park than the Orioles. So far, no sports book that I know of has a line out on grand-slams. The only saving grace for the sports bettor is that this line is only offered on baseball.

FUTURE BETS

At the beginning of a season, any season, the sports books will have all the teams listed on their board with the corresponding odds of winning the pennant, the World Series, The Super Bowl, The NBA Championship, The NCAA, you name it. Technically, the baseball All-Star game is considered a "futures" bet because the line goes up early. In some cases, the bettor can really clean up on long shots, such as the 1985/86 Chicago Bears at 15 to 1 odds. And when the NCAA basketball odds go up just when the 64 teams are announced, look out for the "cinderellas." If you follow college hoops, you know that invariably some unforeseen team makes it to the "Final 4." Nothing scares a sports book more than future bets, which is why the odds against the player are so high.

Incidentally, future bets usually generate the greatest line movement, and provide the bettor with a good reason to shop. But consider these bets only for fun, never for serious money.

SPIT BETS

Some sports books will put up a line on how many times a pitcher spits during a regular 9-inning game. Extra innings don't count. There's also some talk about putting up a "scratch" line. That's right. A line on how many times a pitcher will scratch his . . . ah, crotch. When this line was tried a few years ago, the counter (someone has to count 'em) lost track at 57, and all the bets were returned.

CHAPTER 6

PICKING WINNERS

Your arsenal of weapons to defeat the sports book is severely limited, unless, of course, you're a celebrated TV sports reporter, a team physician, or Carnac The Magnificent. Unlike other forms of gambling, there are no basic and proven strategies to follow, no reams of statistics to ponder. Most statistics are virtually useless as we'll see later in this chapter. And most certainly, the majority of sports handicappers—or sports services as they're better known—are equally worthless and expensive!

MAKE YOUR OWN DECISIONS

Time and time again, your gut instinct will tell you whether or not a spread is too high or too low; if a team is plowed under with problems, or fired up for a big game. You can determine in your own mind if that new quarterback is ready to face a national TV audience; is Seattle really as strong as they looked last week; is the so-called "bitter Rivalry" between Washington and Dallas really what it's cracked up to be; can the Rams play well in the snow; does Kansas City still have a chance for the playoffs?

Indeed, make these decisions yourself. But carefully. Put yourself in the position of the team, and the players. Make your decision without any TV analyst's help, without the sports handicapper's recommendation, and without your friend's bias. But make the decision *only if it's an easy one—an obvious choice.* If not, pass on it and try another game. There's no reason for picking a game other than the fact that for you, it was an easy, obvious decision. *Don't pick a game because it happens to be on TV, and you expect to be home watching it.* That's the worst reason of them all to bet a game. Some players bet a game because their favorite team is playing. That's another bad reason. Still, a few players bet any game without having *any* reason. Just to be "in action" I suppose. For this type of player, I suggest a consultation with his mother-in-law. Someone has to set him straight.

Concentrate on Certain Teams

To make the decisions, it helps of course if you're knowledgeable of the sport. Your local newspaper's sports section is a good source of information, and so are the many fine sports magazines that are available. But remember, in doing so you're looking only for current data, not someone's biased selection.

Equally important, I recommend that you follow a particular team or conference, and consider only those teams for possible betting. If you live in the Midwest and follow the Big Ten, concentrate on only that conference. Forget UCLA or Arkansas if you know little about their team or conference. Sports bettors who are successful follow this important rule of exclusivity. *They give all their effort to a particular team or group of teams, and forget all the others*. Otherwise, there are simply too many teams, too many conferences, and too many players to keep abreast of.

Systems and Statistics

Let's analyze what we've just covered because it's the essence of sports betting.

First, I told you to **ignore any systems or strategies that might have worked in the past**. And that's true, unless you can find someone stupid enough to take your bets on old games, convincing him that you honestly can't remember the scores. Remember, the only time a system works is after the games are over. *Believe me when I tell you that no one will ever be able to devise a system that will work for future games.*

These systems are based on statistics, and that's another area that needs to be discussed. Both systems and statistics are based on prior years and prior events, neither of which have much bearing on today's activity. For example, the Raiders' surprising record on Monday night games is merely a statistical anomaly. Nothing more. Using it as a basis for your decision is a mistake, for so many reasons, not the least of which is the sheer fact that most of the players who were around when the streak began have long since retired.

In so many cases of statistical analysis, years and years of results are fed into a computer and out comes the winner of tonight's game. How foolish! Not only do the players change (especially in college sports), but also the coaches, the managers, and even the cheerleaders . . . if that makes any difference. Even if many players did in fact remain on a particular team over a number of years, chances are their performance has changed, for better or worse, and at the very least they have aged. Nothing stays the same.

As you can see, with all the variables to consider, old statistics might be fun to compile, *but they lend very little to a game's predictability.*

The exception to all of this is of course *current* statistics. That's what I meant by reading newspaper or magazine accounts of particular teams you are following. But even these statistics are chancy at best. A team might start out weak, and finish the year winning their conference. Or a particular team rated high at the beginning of the season, may prove to be a big disappointment.

So-Called "Expert's" Advice

Sports services advertise in national newspapers and magazines, and even now you'll find them touting their selections on cable TV! Although a few might be reputable, many are fly-by-night organizations that pander to the gullible, desperate bettor who thinks of the service as a professional advisor, like an attorney or CPA. Not hardly. Anyone who has monitored these services over the years will know that their records, on average, are at best marginal, and arguably not worth their fee. Of course, there's always the possibility that some sports service will come along and turn up amazing results. But why take the chance? Besides, *a successful year doesn't mean a successful future.* It's the same as statistics and systems. A prognosticator's success last year certainly doesn't guarantee success *this* year. Each new season wipes the slate clean for everyone . . . the team, the player, *and* the analyst.

Pre-Season Predictions

It's fun to pick games, compile current information, listen cautiously to the analysts, and hopefully make a little money along the way. If you like to keep records, try keeping pre-season predictions from all the national magazines and sports experts who'll tell you who's going to win the college football championship, the pennant, the Super Bowl, and so on. This data is widely publicized and generally carries a lot of clout with bettors. All you have to do is keep the records for one season. And you'll never keep them again! When the predictions are made, who's to argue. Who knows if the AP, or Sports Illustrated, or Playboy, Jimmy The Greek, or Beano Cook is right or wrong. But at the end of the season go back to all those predictions and enjoy a good laugh.

The best example of all has to be the 1985 Michigan football Wolverines who were not on anyone's list to go anywhere. They finished the season with a fine 10-1-1 record, including a Fiesta Bowl victory over Nebraska, and had a shot at the number one spot on AP's ranking.

If it's too late to jot down pre-season selections, you can accomplish the same thing by taping any network pre-game show on your VCR. Watch the games and write down the scores. Then play back the tape and listen to the "expert" tell you why the Giants are sure to win. Of course, you'll have already known that the Giants lost 35-zip which makes the "expert" look like the village idiot.

I'm not chastising such prestigious sources as Sports Illustrated, or any celebrated TV analyst. The point is. . . it's tough! Even for the best of them.

This subject reminds me of the TV station down in Texas that recently promoted its football picks by having a chimpanzee actually select the teams. Unless you already know the story, I won't tell you how the chimp did, for fear you'll run out to your neighborhood pet store and order one.

To sum up, stay away from all sources of predictions. Even the "free" ones can be dangerous. In the case of those who charge a fee, understand that they're in it for the money. *Your* money!

The bottom line here is make your own predictions. If all else fails, have your wife make them. You might be *un*pleasantly surprised.

THE LINE ON DISCIPLINE

The most important thing that any author can do for a sports bettor is to try to protect him from himself. Yes, that statement does need some explanation.

Well, we know that any listing of prior year statistics is useless; that's why you won't find team-by-team stats in this book. And we now know that systems are a waste of time too; you won't find any of those in this book either. But what you *will* find that has value is what is about to follow. A "system," if you will, of discipline, money management, and plain common sense. You need it. Everyone needs it. It's protecting yourself from yourself.

Remember to only bet the games that you believe have a decided advantage to you. **Never bet just for the sake of "being in action."** Be disciplined! If you can't get interested in a game unless you have "something riding on it," you have a problem that I can't help. And I'm willing to bet that you lose far more times than you win.

If the game's on TV, watch it and enjoy it, *but don't bet it*. If I'm not getting through, promise me that you'll at least reduce your bet to the absolute minimum limit, but it's still a cop-out. **You must discipline yourself to go with only your strongest picks.** If you've looked at the lines and the entire weekend looks bleak, don't even open your wallet.

A tough example of this rule is the Monday night game during football season, the only game of the day. If it's a tough pick, pass! "Yes," you say, "but I'm going to be watching it!" So watch it! But don't bet it.

Still a better example of this pitfall is the Super Bowl, the last game of the season. Everyone has to bet it, right? Wrong! Not if it's a bad bet for you. If the point-spread is about where you would place it, and you can't move off center, enjoy the Super Bowl but (all in unison) DON'T BET IT!

The Super Bowl is a tough test of a bettor's discipline for other reasons too. Since it's the last game of the season, it might be a good chance to recoup your season losses, right? Maybe. Maybe not. If you're on the wrong side of the ledger, stay small, *don't try to recoup previous losses with one reckless bet*. Accept the fact that you've had a losing season and be done with it. The smart bettor, whether in the casino, at the race track, or in a sports stadium, follows this cardinal rule of betting: **Lay back when you're losing, but let your winnings run.** Never increase your bets when you're in the red; in fact, that's the time to reduce your wagers or quit. Let any winnings build safely, and increase the bets as you continue to win. It should be obvious, but *only a few gamblers have the discipline to structure their bets in relation to their winnings or losses.* Not only does the strength of the game determine the size of your bet, so does your season "standing" at that time. Are you "up," or are you "down"? Win or lose, it's a critical factor in determining your bet size.

VULNERABILITY

Not only must you be careful of your selections and careful of your bet size, but you must also be careful of your vulnerability. Let's say for example that you are going to bet four games next Sunday . . . four football games that you particularly like. For sake of example, let's say that each game is played at $100. Although you can't possibly believe that you might lose all four games, your vulnerability for that day *is* $400. If losing one or two hundred won't hurt you, but losing four hundred might sting a little, you're not using common sense. In fact, sting or no sting, it's not a good move and here's why. Regardless of how good your picks are, you might lose all four games. In fact, it's a statistical certainty that you will indeed lose four out of four games eventually, if you continually play four at a time. Without regard to any skill in your selection, the odds are 15 to 1 that you will lose all four (and your temper).

But more than that, betting all four games at once precludes you from structuring your bet size as your results become known. If the four games were bet over four different sessions, you could increase your bets if you win the first game, then the second, etc., or reduce your bets if you lost the first, the second, etc. By dumping all your action on one shot, you've prevented yourself from making any adjustment to your bet size.

Fractioning your total bet among four, five, or even

six games is no assurance against anything. You're on the hook, and there *are* upsets. Be careful!

Greed Turns Winners Into Losers

It's important to note that most pro bettors go with one or two games per football weekend, maybe three at the most, and only then if the picks are all very, very strong. Are you that disciplined, or are you just a touch greedy? Are you mesmerized by the pleasant thought of winning all eight out of the eight games you just picked? Did you think about losing all eight?

Greed is the bookie's ally. Greed turns winners into losers. Be satisfied with a small, modest win, and start preparing for the next batch of games next week. No? You say that Sunday's early games are now over and you won two out of three. Now the late games are up and since you're ahead a little you might as well pick another one—a game that didn't particularly hit you at the start of the day. Three out of four sounds a lot better than two out of three, huh? Are you getting greedy? Are you betting recklessly? I wish I could take all of your action.

Actually, I don't. What I do wish however, is that you find the discipline to bet smartly and manage your money properly. Above all, **never make a bet that you can't comfortably afford to lose**. I said, *"Comfortably."* That doesn't mean having to hock the family car. You've heard it before and now you're hearing it again. It's the most important rule to follow. STAY WITHIN YOUR MEANS.

CHAPTER 7

SECRETS OF A PRO BETTOR

The logical questions that come up when you try to define a successful sports bettor are: "How do they do it? What do they look for? What are their secrets of winning?" Good questions!

We've learned throughout this book that they must be both an expert at the games and an expert at betting; they must consider only current statistics; and avoid the temptation of using "systems," or advice from touters or TV personalities who think *they* are the experts.

But these points, although important, are not really "secrets." So let's analyze some of the "strategies" that many pro bettors believe are the secrets of their success.

STUDY THE PLAYERS

In basketball, a good study of the starting players is far more beneficial to the sports bettor than in any other sport. Why? *One player is 20% of the team on the floor!* If a bettor's research shows that a key player tends to play poorly in certain arenas (and this does happen) then the bettor has found a possible advantage over the bookmaker. Of course, if the oddsmaker knew the same thing the bettor knows, that factor will be built into the line, assuming the oddsmaker believes a large portion of the betting public is aware of it also.

In basketball, a sharp bettor who knows his business will spend considerable time on each individual player, more so than on the aggregate team, to try to find out things that the oddsmaker overlooked. The bettor will look beyond publicized injuries, reported disputes with the coach or other players, that sort of thing. What he's really looking for are personal things, such as a pending divorce that's not in the papers, a minor sickness, unreported financial problems, drugs, or even problems with the player's kids. Information of this type might seem difficult to acquire, but not really. The pro bettor has many contacts critical to his success and called upon often.

In baseball, there's no question that the pitchers get the most attention from the fans . . . and from the successful sports bettors too. Any decent bettor must study the pitchers carefully, for they have more influence on the line, and on your wagers, than any other factor.

Generally, the successful bettor is only interested in the pitcher's last three or four outings. Notice I said "the last three," not the last ten. The bettor should not even care about the early part of a season if he's nearing the playoffs. Pitchers change over the course of a season, as do all players. *What the bettor is looking for is a trend to consider, a trend that is timely and relevant to the upcoming game.* For those who don't keep such detailed records, many large newspapers routinely publish the listed pitchers and their records over the last three games. In most cases, the betting lines are also shown.

Similarly, football bettors will keep the same type of records about a quarterback's performance over the past three or four games. Trends of prior years are clearly of no interest, but trends over the past three games are obviously critical in predicting the quarterback's upcoming performance. No guarantees, mind you, but a telling trend that might, just might, continue.

The same factors that we cited earlier are also appropriate for the pitcher or quarterback as an individual, key player. His performance in certain stadiums, his mental attitude, personal problems, dissentions, etc., must never be discounted.

LINE BIAS

Another area of concern to the pro bettor deals with "regional" and "emotional" factors that might be plugged into a betting line. For example, oddsmakers know that San Francisco teams might be overly favored in Reno betting parlors, and similarly, Los Angeles teams in Las Vegas. If the bettor believes a line is unduly favored by a regional bias, he might be able to take advantage of the discrepancy. And then there are teams that always seem to get favorable attention . . . the sports bettor's "pets" so to speak. Teams such as Notre Dame, Dallas Cowboys, Chicago Bears, and even the Atlanta Hawks because of their cable network affiliation, tend to receive more than their share of favoritism. Such emotional factors can also become an advantage to the shrewd sports bettor who can detect the bias in the oddsmaker's lines.

And speaking of lines, many bettors are careful to watch for a movement in a line. If a line is moving away from his pending selection, he might talk with a sports book manager, or with other experienced bettors to find out why. Just as the sports book manager confers with other managers to strengthen and "tune in" a betting line, so do the bettors themselves who treat it seriously.

The experienced bettor knows that the bulk of factors that might lend predictability to the game have most likely been already applied to the opening line. Factors such as home-team underdogs (a favorite of unsuspecting bettors), West Coast to East Coast travel, let-downs, big games, interstate rivalries, etc., are almost always accounted for in the making of a line. Just knowing that puts the avid bettor at an advantage, by not applying the factor twice, or simply by knowing that the factor shouldn't have been counted in the first place.

BLOW-OUTS

A great many bettors concentrate on the non-conference college basketball and football schedule (the early season games) knowing that the oddsmakers are usually prevented from putting up "team-accurate" lines for likely blowouts. Either the games go off the betting board or the numbers simply are not enough. Maybe the lines are correct for dividing the bettors as they are supposed to do, but not high enough to accurately reflect the playing potential of two mismatched teams. If you're not afraid to give 30 points (the pro bettor isn't) you might find another "plum" in the oddsmaker's lines. If you're in doubt about this phenomena, read the college scores in the sports section Sunday morning, look for the mismatches, then look at the spreads and form your own conclusion. *For many bettors, these mismatches are money in the bank.*

Another trait of the seasoned bettor is in identifying

the weakest lines among the different sports to be offered. In Barney Vinson's excellent book about the gambling scene, *Las Vegas Behind The Tables,* the author states, ''It's been said that the really pro bettors concentrate on basketball, both pro and college, and on college football. It's also said that what the sports books lose on Saturday college football, they more than make up for on Sunday pro action. Apparently, the pros are less predictable.''

It couldn't be said any better. **Most bookmakers agree that the weakest lines, in order, are: (1) early season college basketball, (2) college football, (3) pro basketball, (4) baseball, (5) pro football.** And *you* probably spend most of your money, literally, knocking heads with the pros on Sunday!

The theory behind the listing also relates to what we covered earlier—the likelihood of mismatches and blowouts. The parity among the pros is virtually a year-in, year-out affair. With the usual exceptions of course. The old axiom, ''On any given Sunday . . .'' does prove our point. Most any team is capable of beating any other. But try that out on UCLA vs. Utah State! The point is, Tampa Bay might not be the best team in the NFL but the team is made up of *pros!* Stand-outs in college. How the hell can you pick them?

BET SIZE

Although it's more a ''money management'' trait than a strategy, the size of the pro bettor's wager should be mentioned at this point. In a way, the structuring of bets can be considered a pro bettor's secret since they all have their own idiosyncrasies. *Most bettors will compute the size of their next wagers after a careful plot of their win expectancy, based on their original stake and win/lose balances to date.* To most of them, their methods are a proprietary matter. Nonetheless, we can assume that most of them follow the "Kelly Criterion" or an off-shoot of the formula that suggests the correct betting amounts based on a desired win percentage, original investment, number of bets, and anticipated earnings.

If you're starting with a $5,000 bankroll, it makes no sense to wager $2,500 on the first weekend of football. A wipe-out that weekend wipes out half of your stake! That's called the "Stupid Criterion," and works rather well if you're into charity.

As a general rule, the smart bettor will wager no more than 3 or 4% of his original stake, based on a realistic winning percentage of maybe 57%. Any more than that is pure "pie in the sky."* Yes, just recognizing that fact is also the mark of a tough bettor . . . recognizing that he's not infallible. If you won three out of three this past weekend it doesn't mean you're invincible, it just means you did your homework. Hopefully, it didn't mean you were lucky. Luck doesn't make it in any form of gambling.

Another mark of a successful sports bettor is knowing when he's hot! And cashing it in for all it's worth. Like anything else, winners and losers in the sports bet-

---

*In football or basketball, the bettor will break even against the point-spread by winning 52.3% of his games, assuming all bets are at the same level. That important percentage is easy to prove. Since the bettor must lay 11 to 10 odds, winning 11 games over the course of 21 yields our break even point: $11/21 = .523 = 52.3\%$. In a more empirical fashion, winning 11 games at $100 nets $1,100, and losing 10 games at $100 costs us $1,100 ($1,000 plus $100 juice).

There are only a few documented cases of a bettor winning more than 60% over the course of a season. As you can now see, any winning percentage over 52.3% can be considered successful.

tor's record books come in streaks sometimes, and most often the streaks are tied to the bettor's proficiency at that particular time. A good streak-bettor, who's far ahead in the season already, might veer from his regimentized betting criteria and begin increasing his wagers 30 to 60%. He knows he's on the right track, betting back his winnings in pursuit of greater profits. Making large wagers when you're well ahead is the *only* time to do this. "Strike when the iron's hot," "Make hay while the sun shines," "When you're hot you're hot!" All these neat little phrases that mean the same thing do indeed apply here. The trick is having the determination, and the guts, to see it through. It might be easy betting $100 on a football game. But $200? $300? If you're up considerably (and I mean *considerably)*, and a loss won't hurt you beyond your original expectations, yes, now's the time to increase the size of your wagers.

But streaks won't last forever. When it ends, count your winnings, go back to your original betting plans, and wait for another ride up.

Incidentally, this point reminds me of a common phrase that's heard around sports betting circles, "I'm in good shape, I'm betting with the bookie's money." NO! Your winnings are *your* money. Not the bookie's. That attitude can only lead to reckless, senseless losses. Your winnings are *your* money. It bears repeating.

Good Luck!